Thank you!

Hey Parents,

As a way of saying thanks for buying this book, I'm offering a FREE printable story-based adventure—**Mission to the Moon**!

In this fun-filled activity, kids will complete mini-challenges to launch their rocket, land on the moon, and return safely to Earth! Along the way, they'll enjoy: Coloring (boosting creativity and fine motor skills) and they will be looking for Clues & Solving Games (encouraging problem-solving, patience, and focus).

These activities make learning exciting, keeping kids engaged while they develop important cognitive and motor skills—without even realizing it!

Open the camera on your phone (as if you're going to take a photo), hold the phone over the QR code, then a link will appear on your screen. Tap on the link to get your free download!

A FREE GIFT FOR YOU!

Welcome to Your Space Adventure!

Get ready to explore the wonders of the universe with this exciting activity book! Designed for young space explorers like you, this book is packed with fun and engaging activities to spark your curiosity about space. From coloring rockets and planets to solving mazes and connecting the dots, each page is an adventure waiting to be discovered.

How to Use This Book:

🚀 **Find Your Space Station:** Pick a cozy spot where you can focus and let your imagination soar.

✏️ **Grab Your Gear:** Use crayons, markers, or colored pencils to bring the pages to life with bright, bold colors!

Complete the Activities:

- **Dot-to-Dot:** Connect the numbers to reveal cool space-themed images.
- **Space Dot Markers:** Fill in the shapes with colorful dots to create cosmic artwork.
- **Scissor Skills:** Carefully cut along the lines to practice using scissors—ask an adult for help if needed!
- **"Did You Know?" Facts:** Fun space facts that make learning exciting and memorable.
- **Mazes:** Guide astronauts and spaceships through tricky paths in space.
-

Let Your Imagination Take Off! There's no wrong way to enjoy this book—just have fun, be creative, and explore the universe your way!

Are you ready for lift-off?

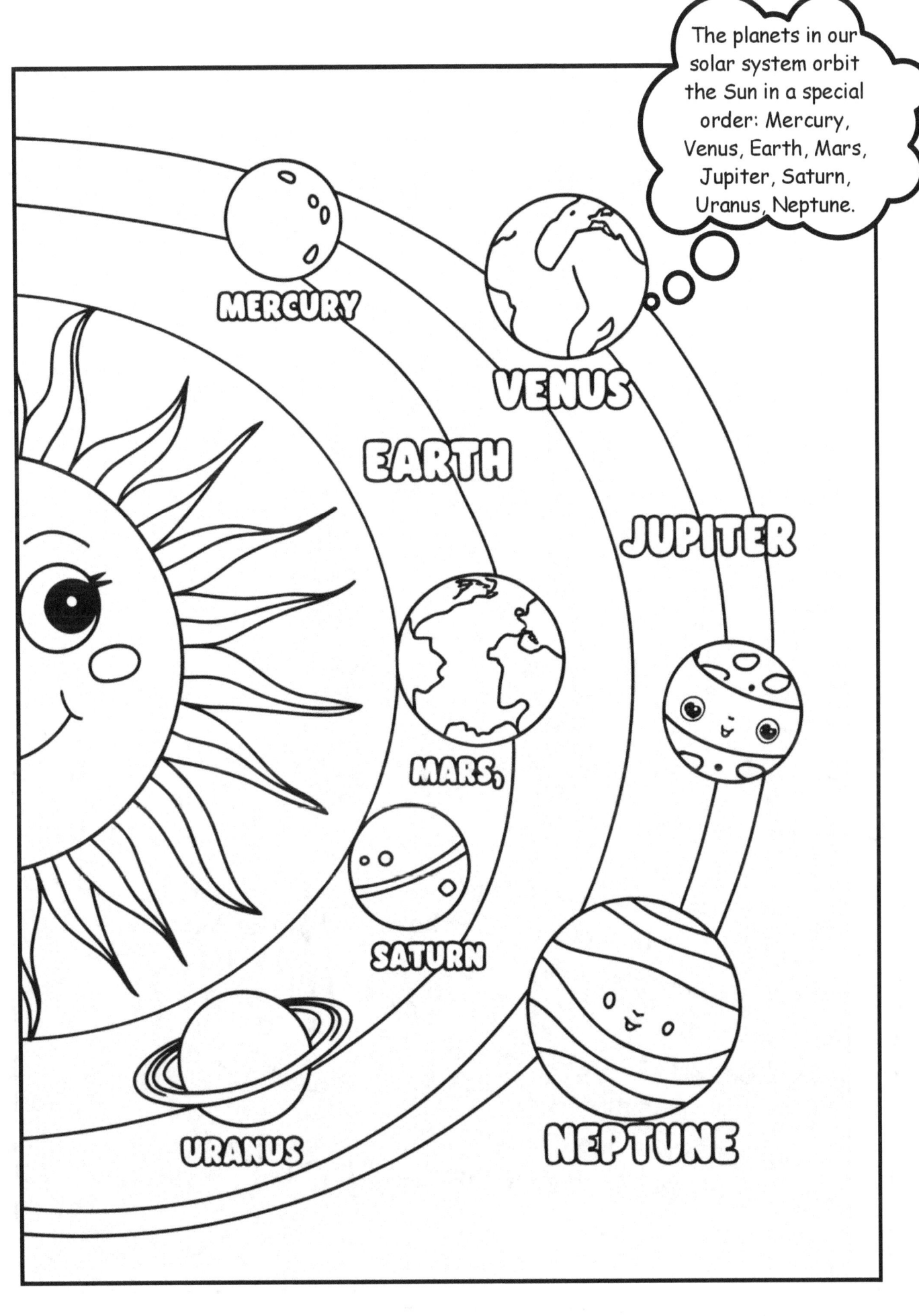

WELCOME, SPACE EXPLORER!

Welcome to a brand-new planet! It's full of exciting new creatures that you've never seen before.
Your mission is to design your very own alien. What does it look like? Is it big or small? Does it have multiple eyes, legs, or arms? Maybe it can fly or even change colors!

DESIGN YOUR OWN ALIEN!

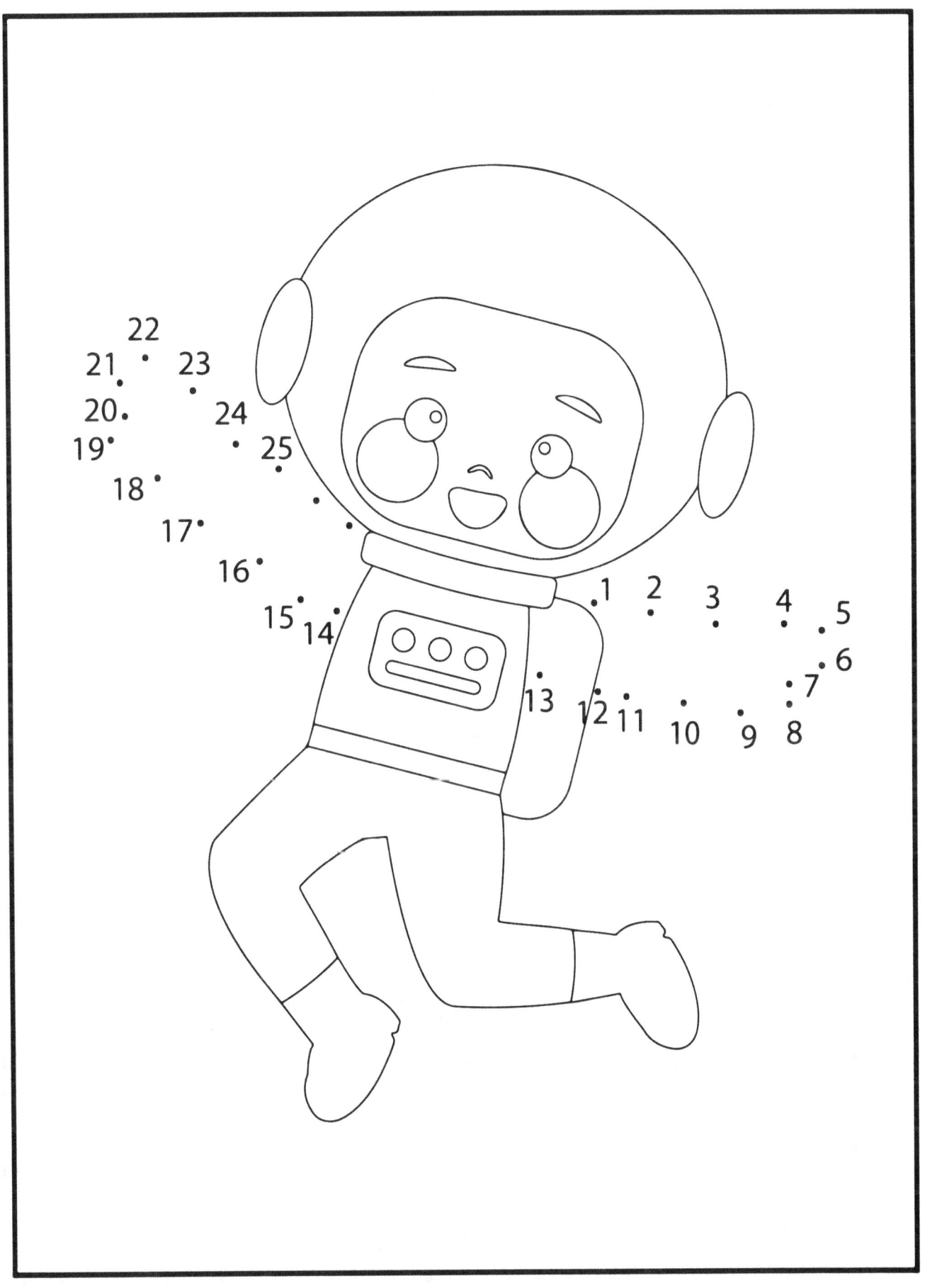

How To Draw Space

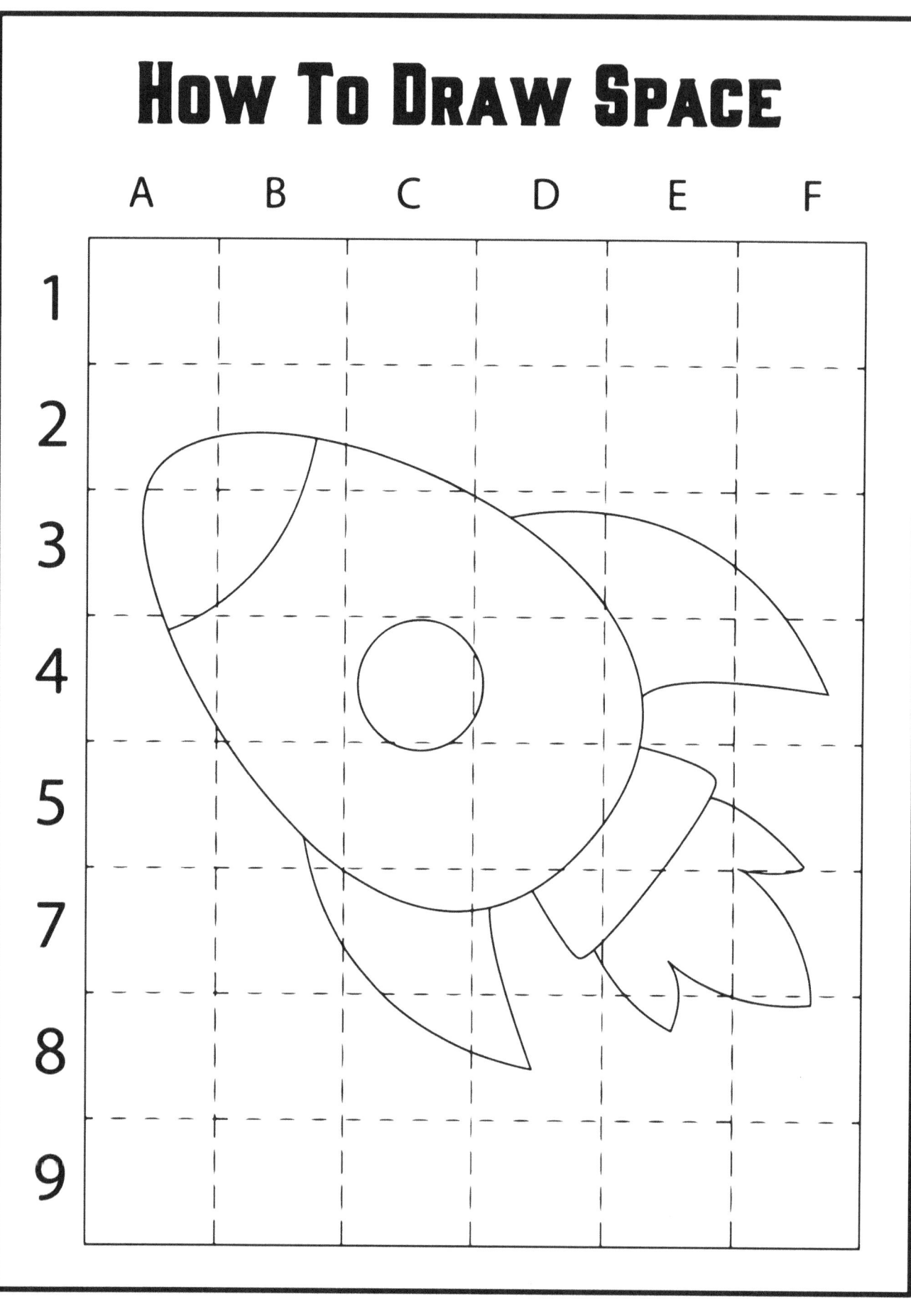

Your Turn!

	A	B	C	D	E	F
1						
2						
3						
4						
5						
7						
8						
9						

Help the astronaut find his way back to the rocket!

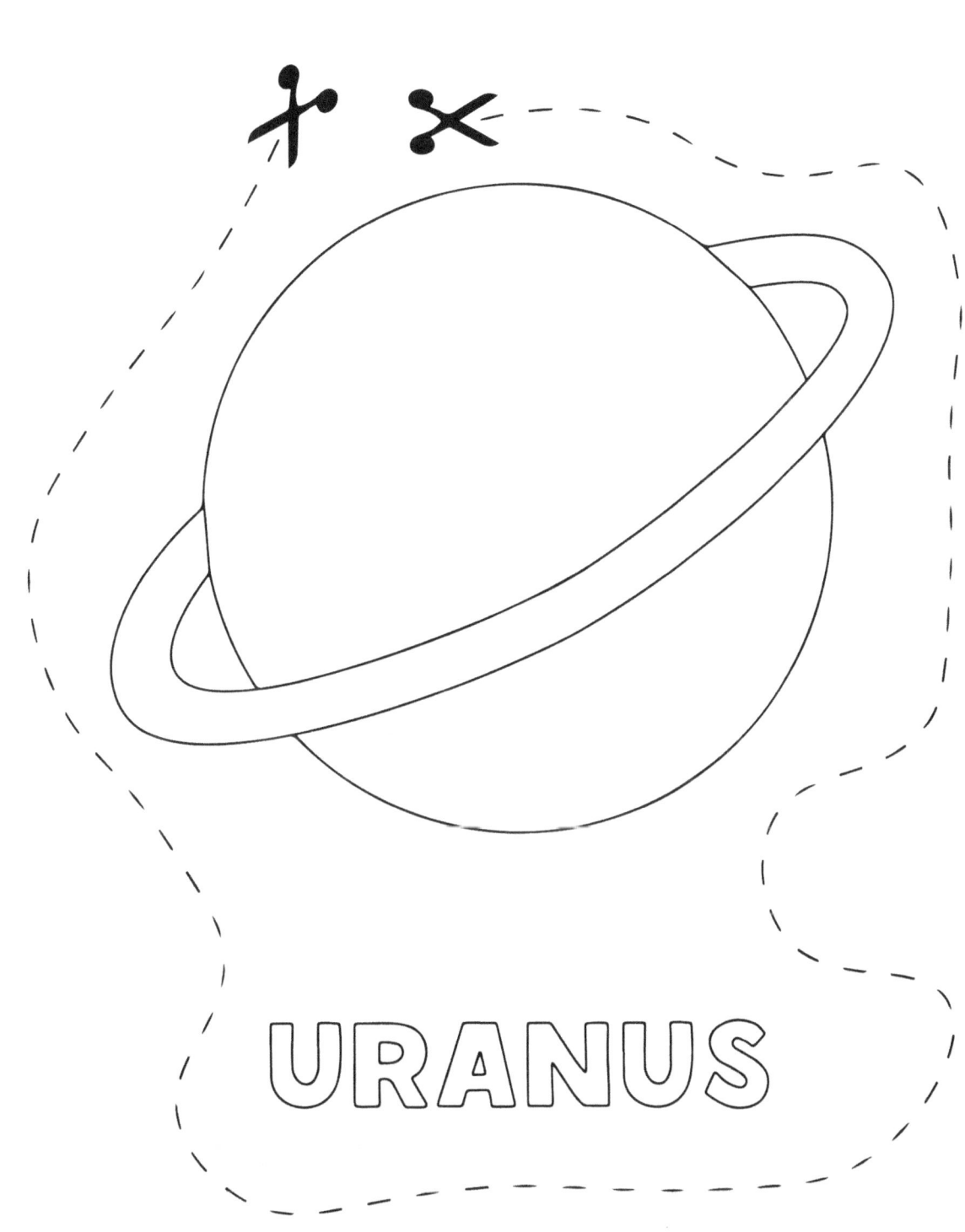

URANUS

URANUS

DID YOU KNOW?

Did you know that Uranus **spins on its side like a rolling ball?** Unlike most planets, which spin like a top, Uranus is tilted almost completely sideways! Scientists think a giant space rock crashed into it a long time ago, knocking it over. This means that **for 42 years, one side of Uranus is in darkness, while the other side has nonstop sunlight!**

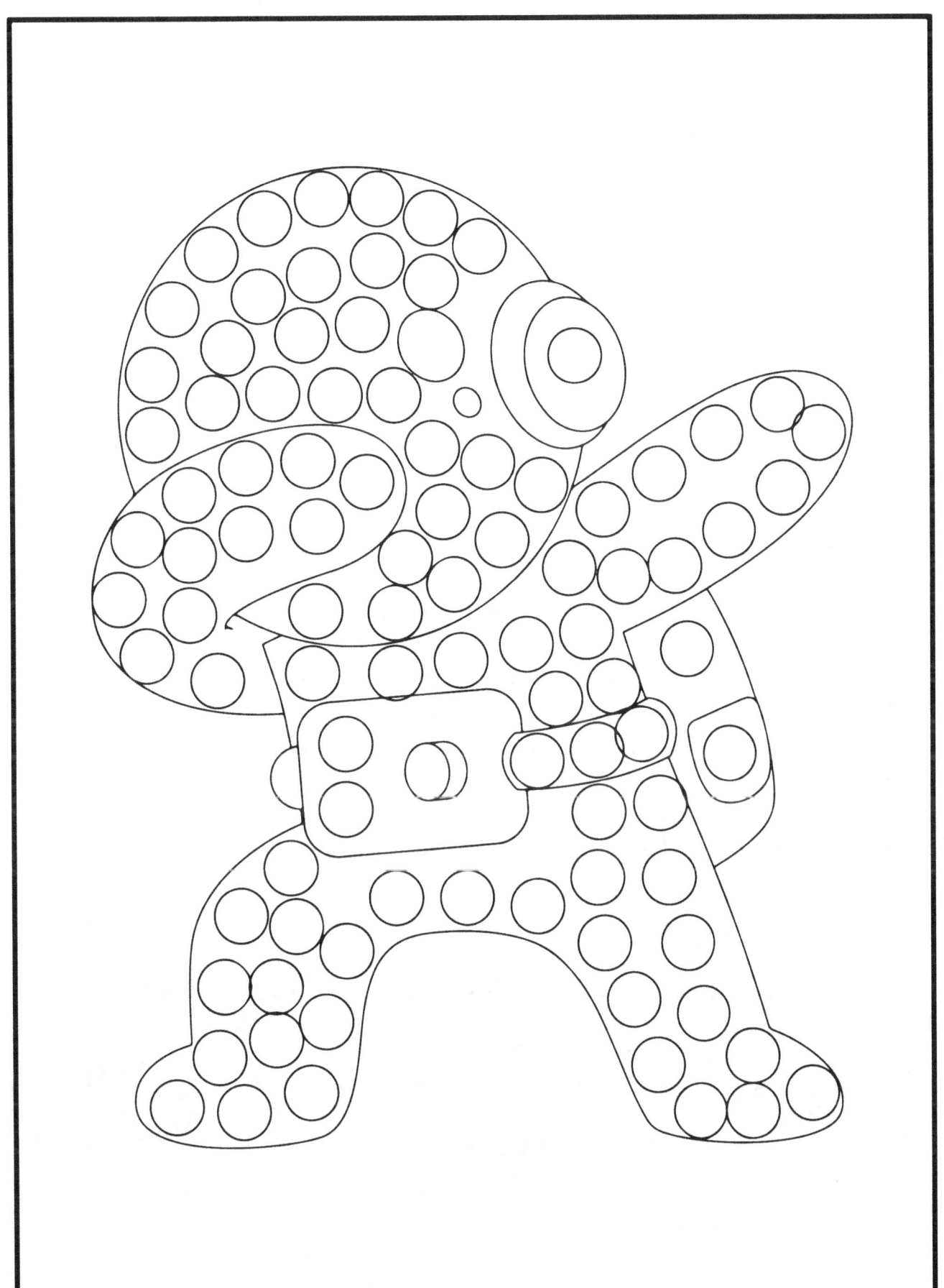

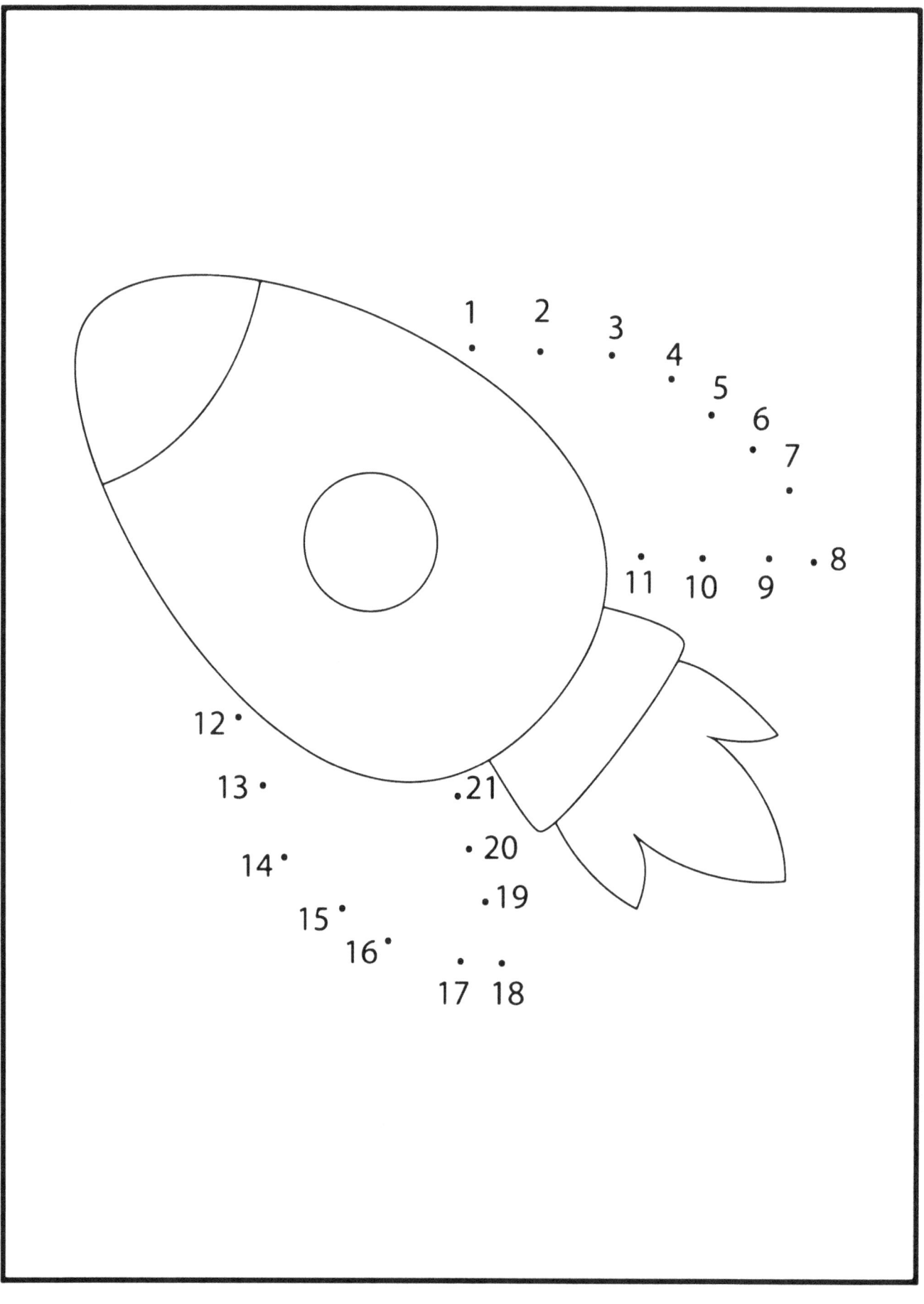

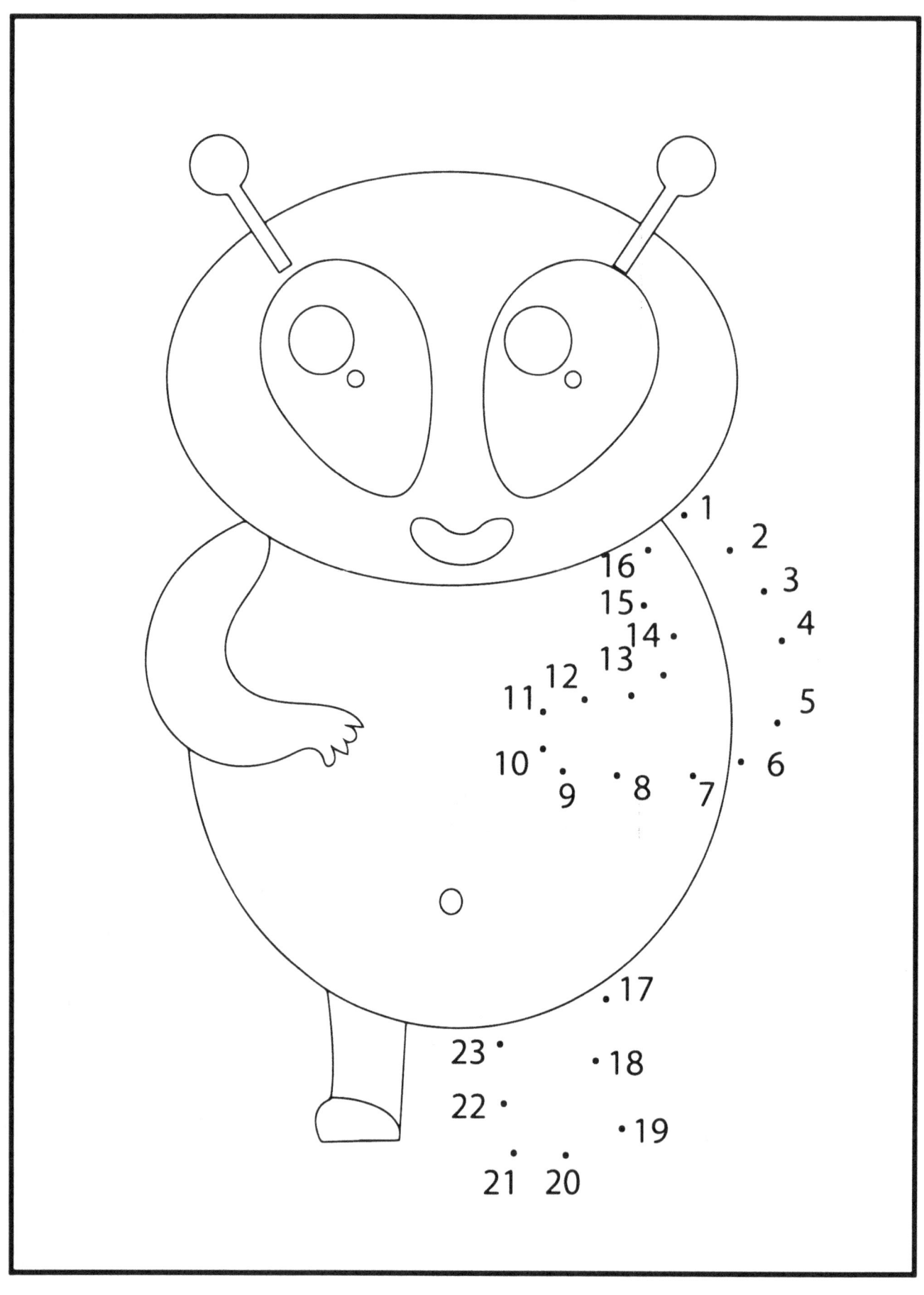

HOW TO DRAW SPACE

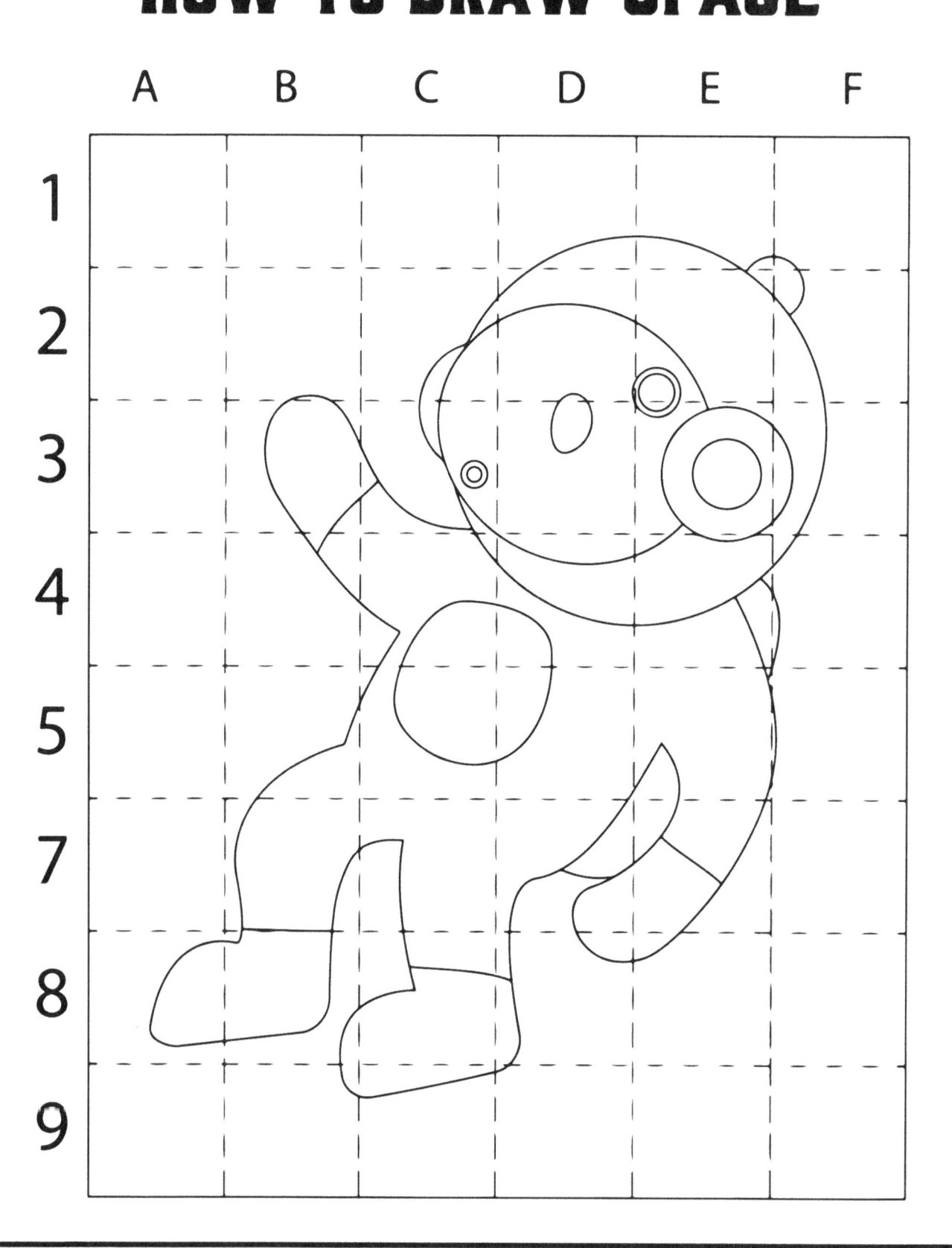

YOUR TURN!

	A	B	C	D	E	F
1						
2						
3						
4						
5						
7						
8						
9						

DID YOU KNOW?

Did you know that the Sun is **so big** you could fit **one million Earths** inside it? It's like a giant, fiery ball in space, always shining and keeping us warm. Without the Sun, there would be no life on Earth!

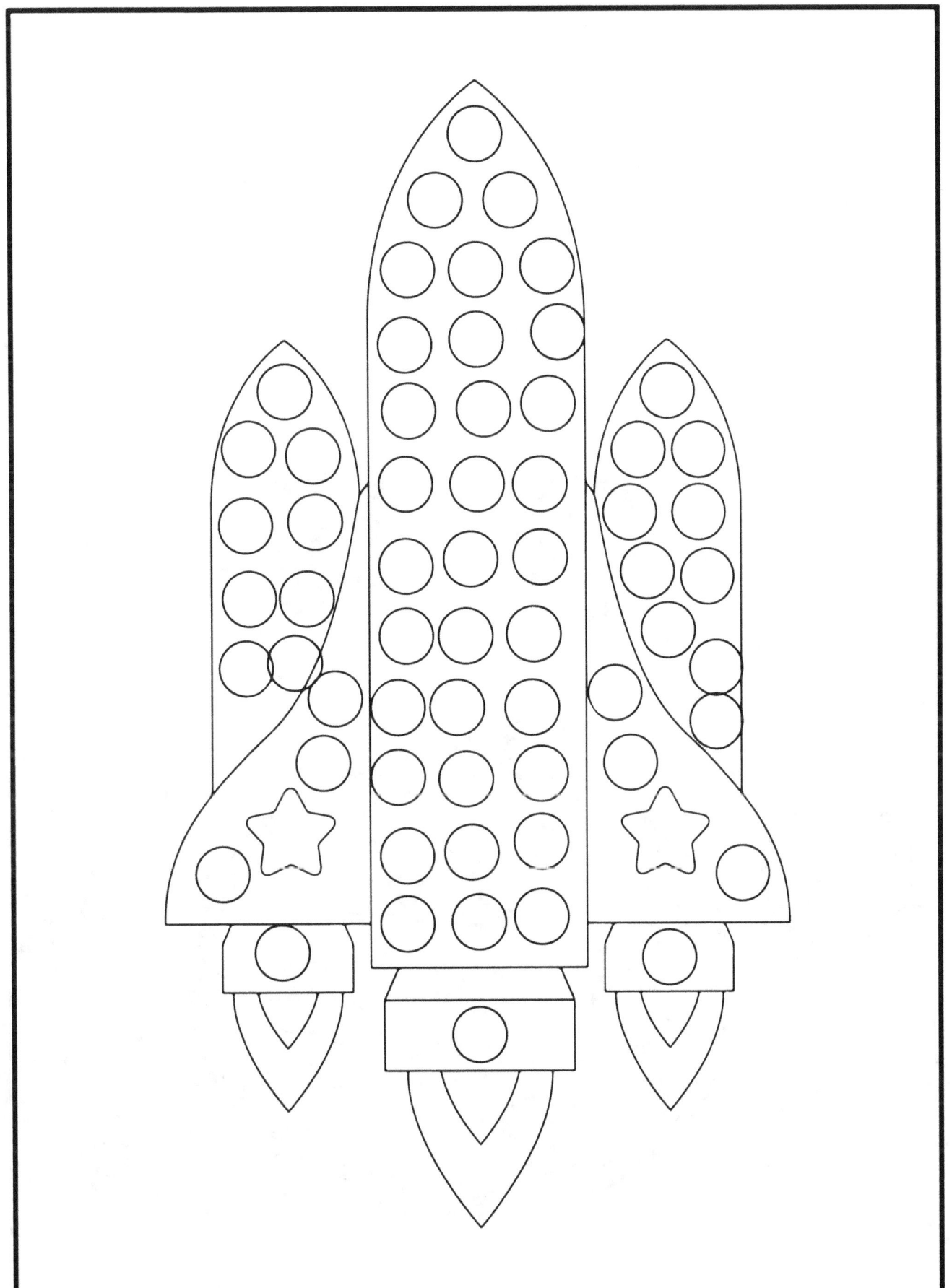

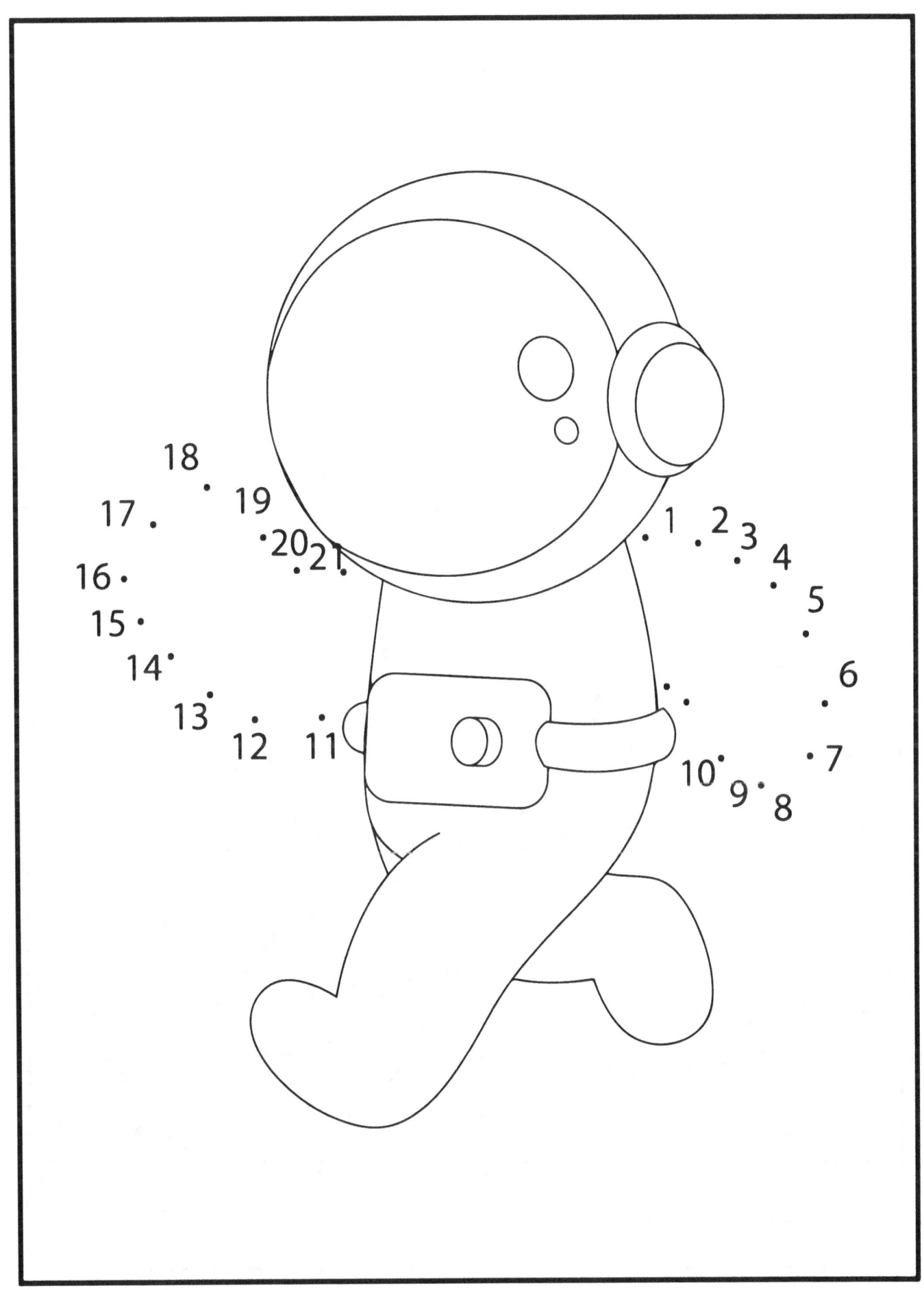

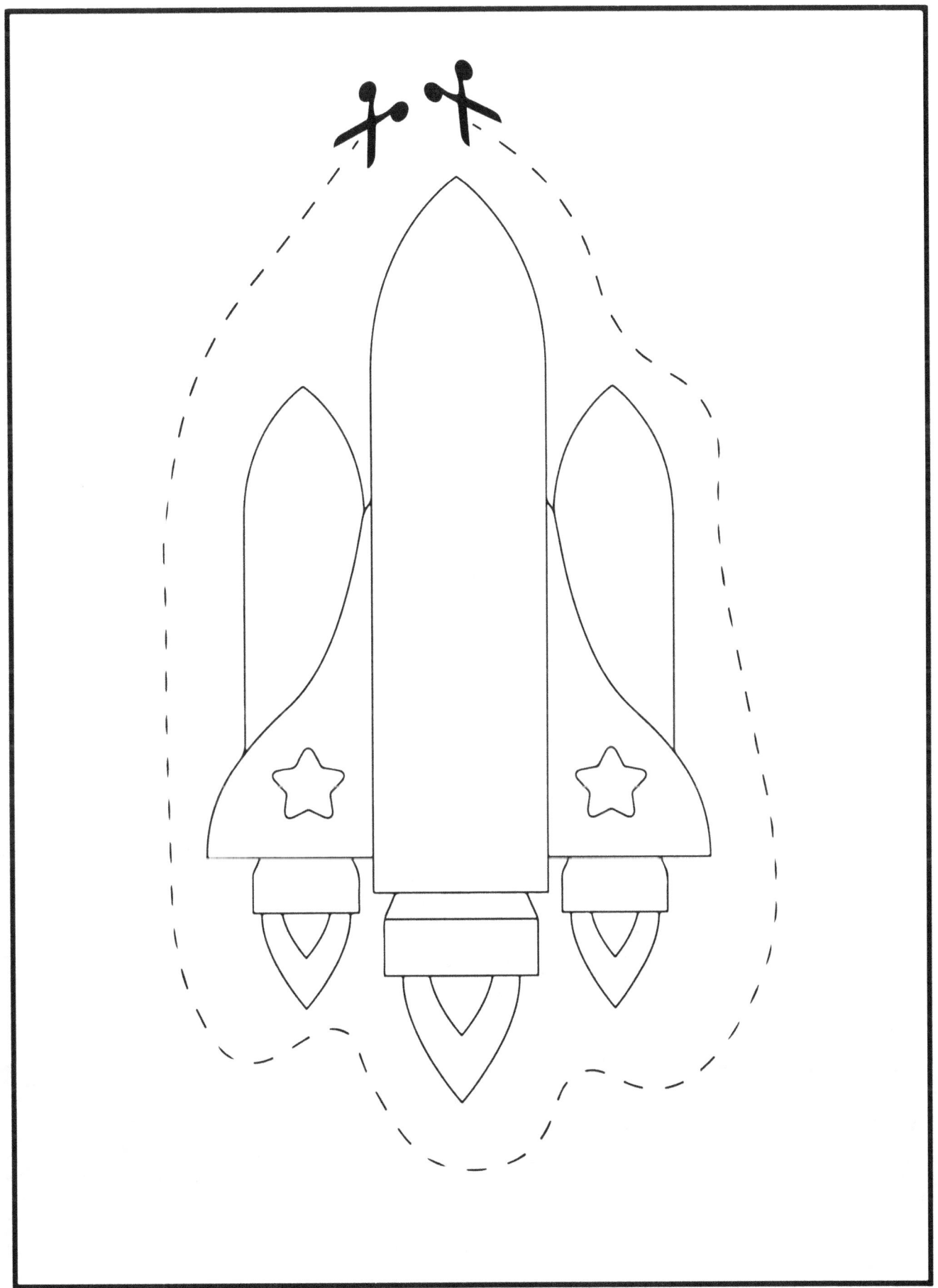

DID YOU KNOW?

Did you know that **spaceships don't need wheels** because there's no gravity in space? Instead of driving, they **float and zoom** using powerful rocket engines! Astronauts inside have to **strap themselves in so they don't float away!**

HOW TO DRAW SPACE

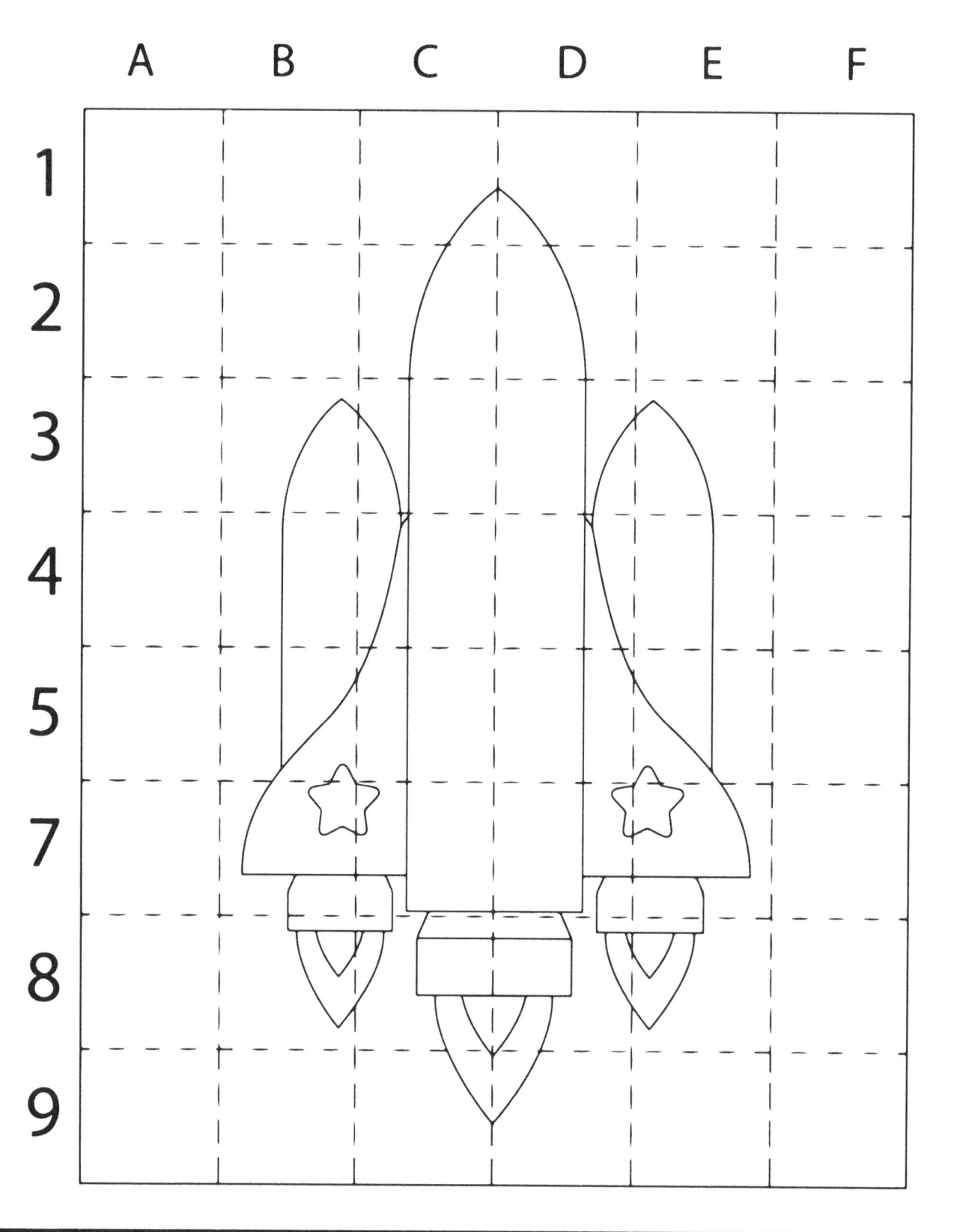

YOUR TURN!

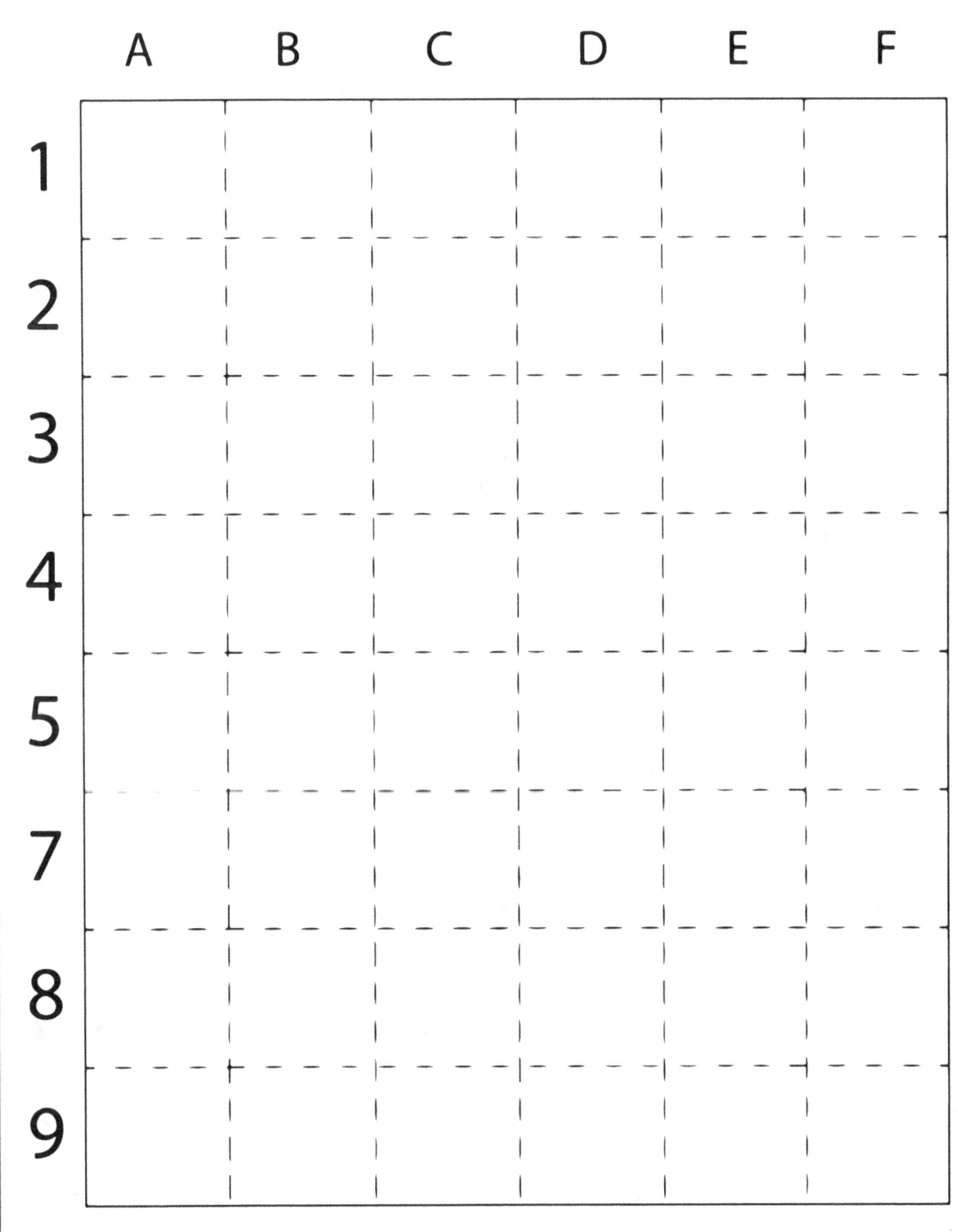

	A	B	C	D	E	F
1						
2						
3						
4						
5						
7						
8						
9						

Build Your Own Space Story

One day, an astronaut named _____
traveled to _____ and discovered a _____.
It was _____!

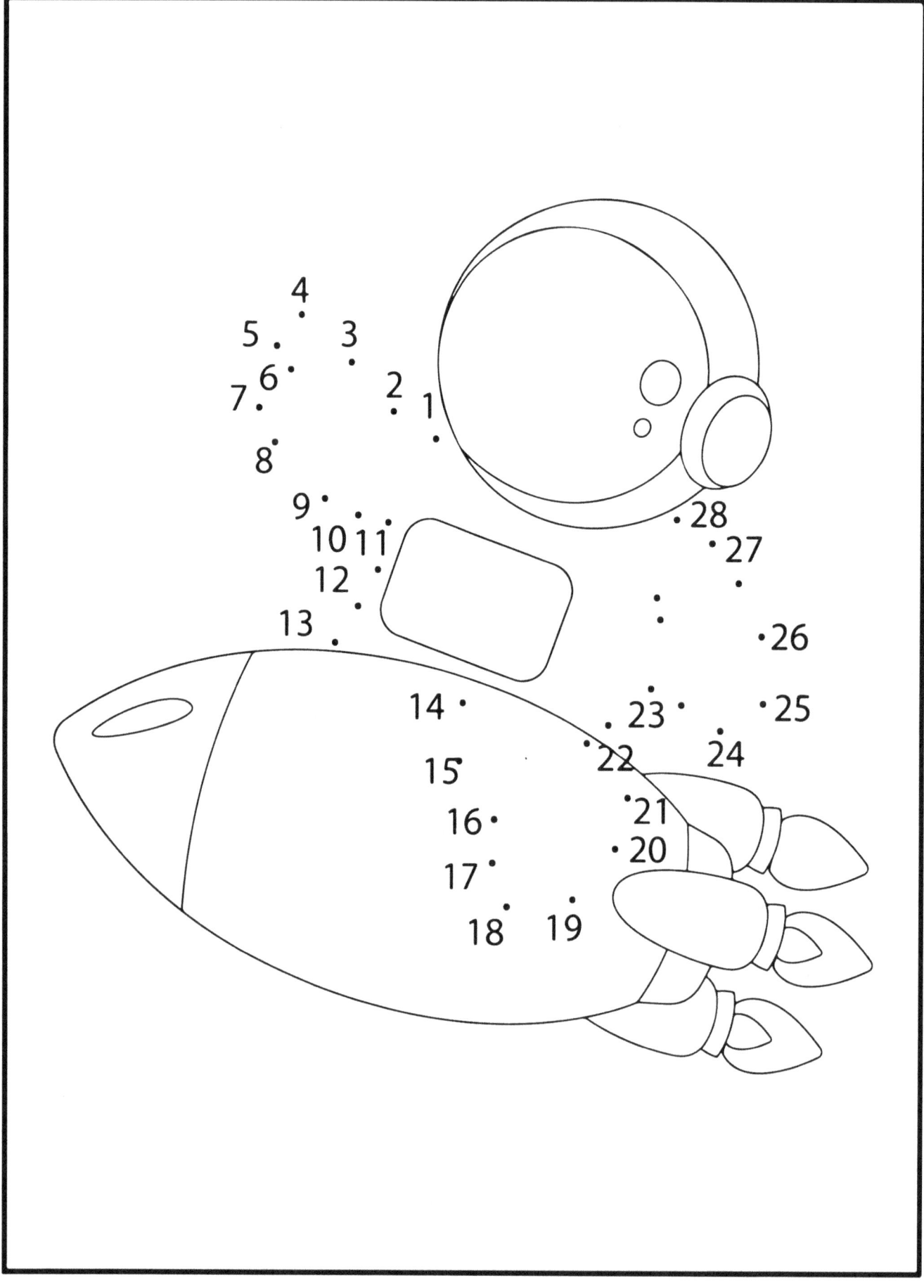

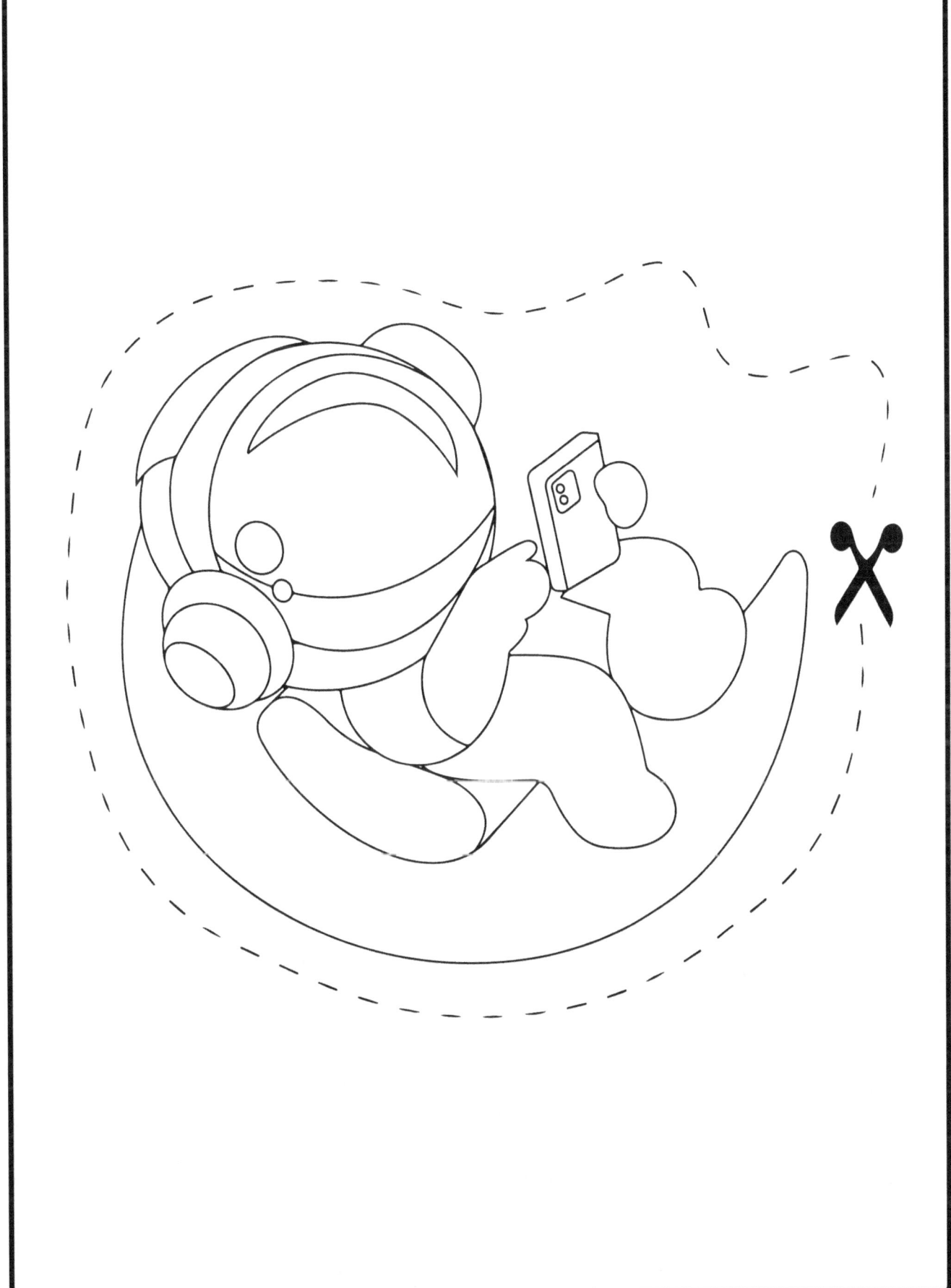

DID YOU KNOW?

Did you know that **in space, you can't hear any sounds?** That's because space has no air, and sound needs air to travel. So if you shouted in space, no one would hear you—even if you were right next to them! But don't worry—astronauts talk to each other using special radios inside their helmets!

Did you know?

Did you know that the first people to walk on the Moon left **their footprints there forever**? Since **the Moon has no wind or rain**, the footprints from the **Apollo astronauts in 1969** are still there today—and they might stay for millions of years!

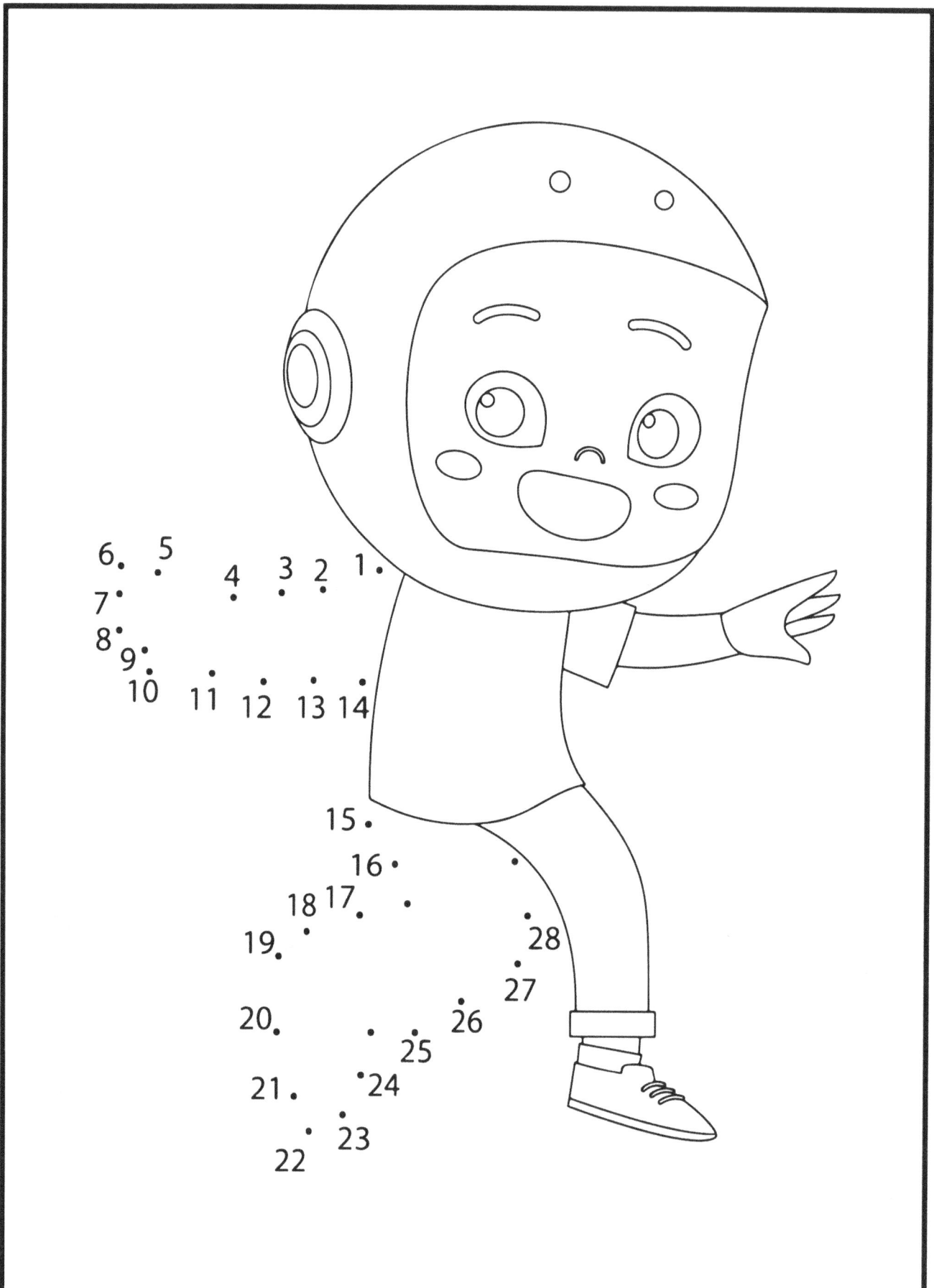

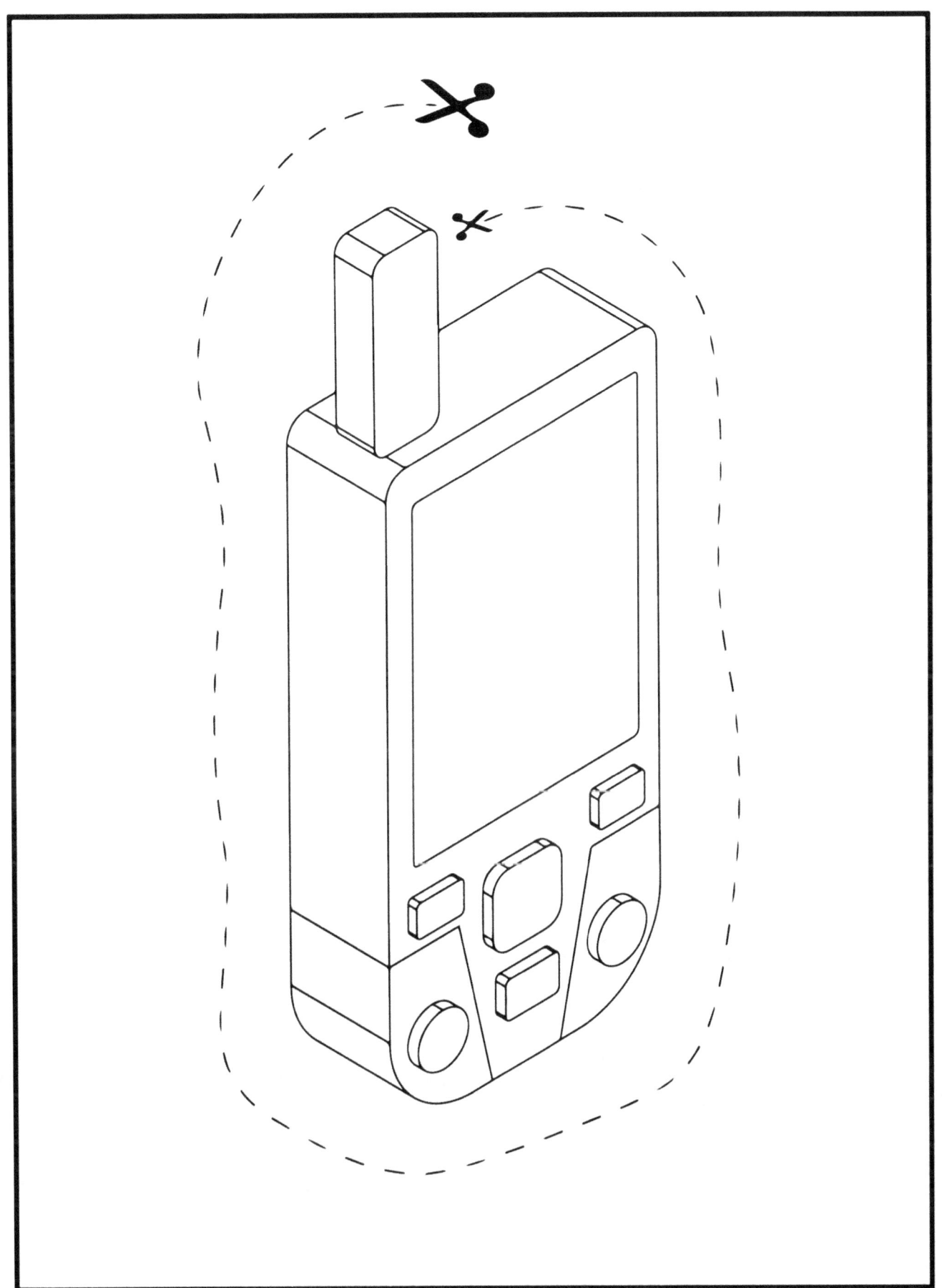

SATURN

DID YOU KNOW?

Did you know that **Saturn has giant rings made of ice and rock?** They're so big, you could fit seven Earths inside the space between Saturn and its rings! The rings are really wide, but they're only about as thick as a house—so thin, even though they look huge!

How To Draw Space

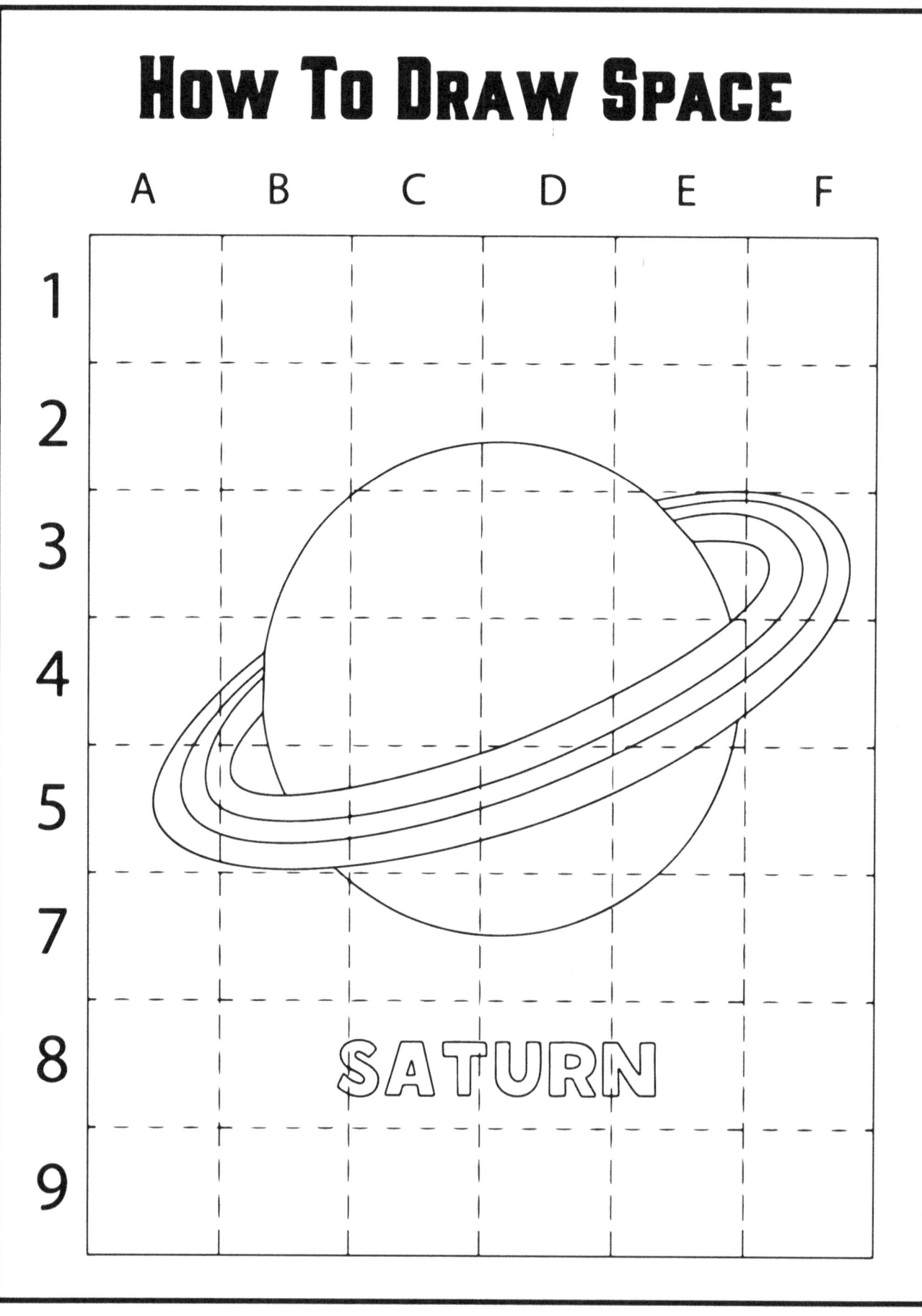

YOUR TURN!

	A	B	C	D	E	F
1						
2						
3						
4						
5						
7						
8						
9						

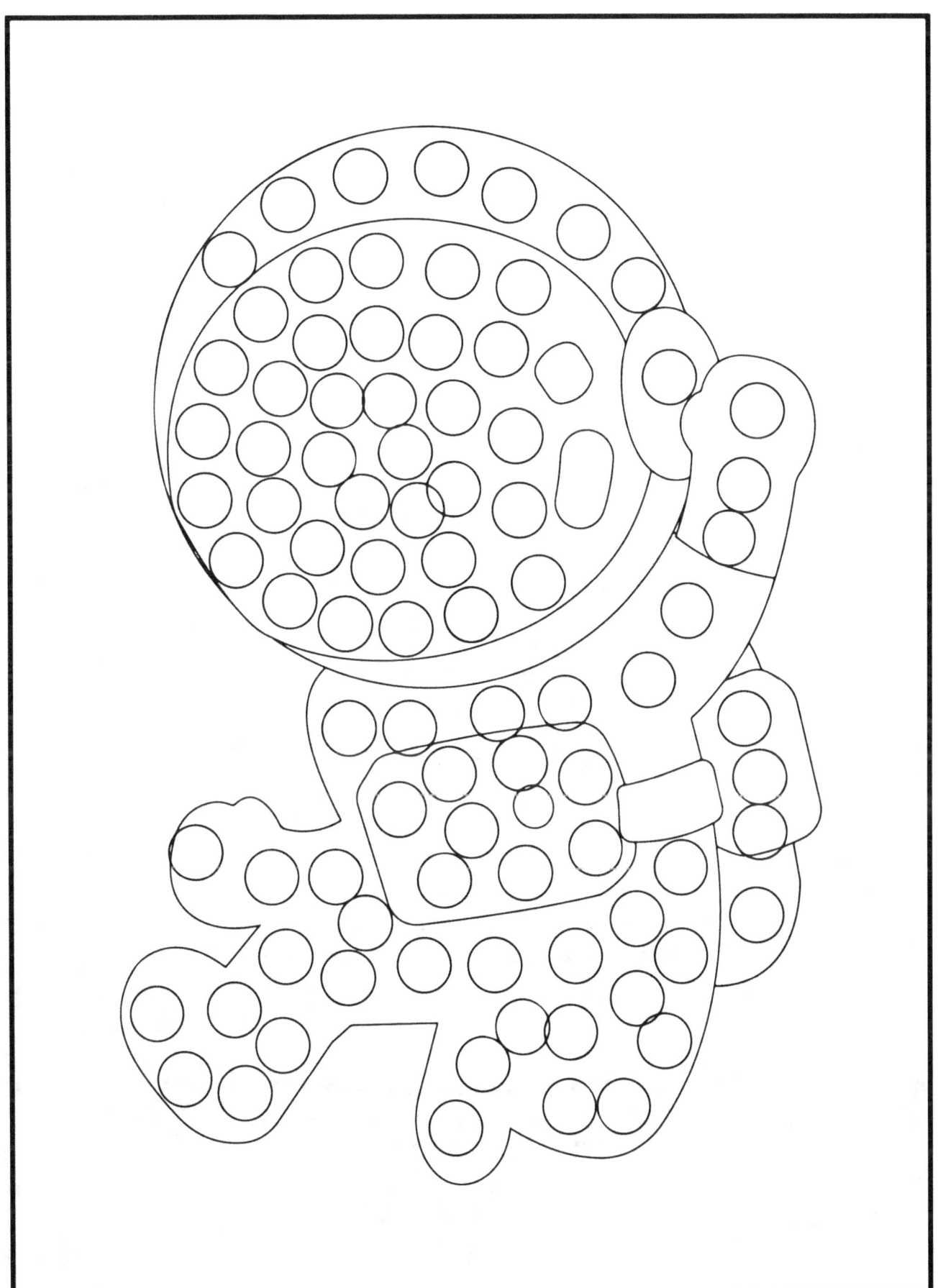

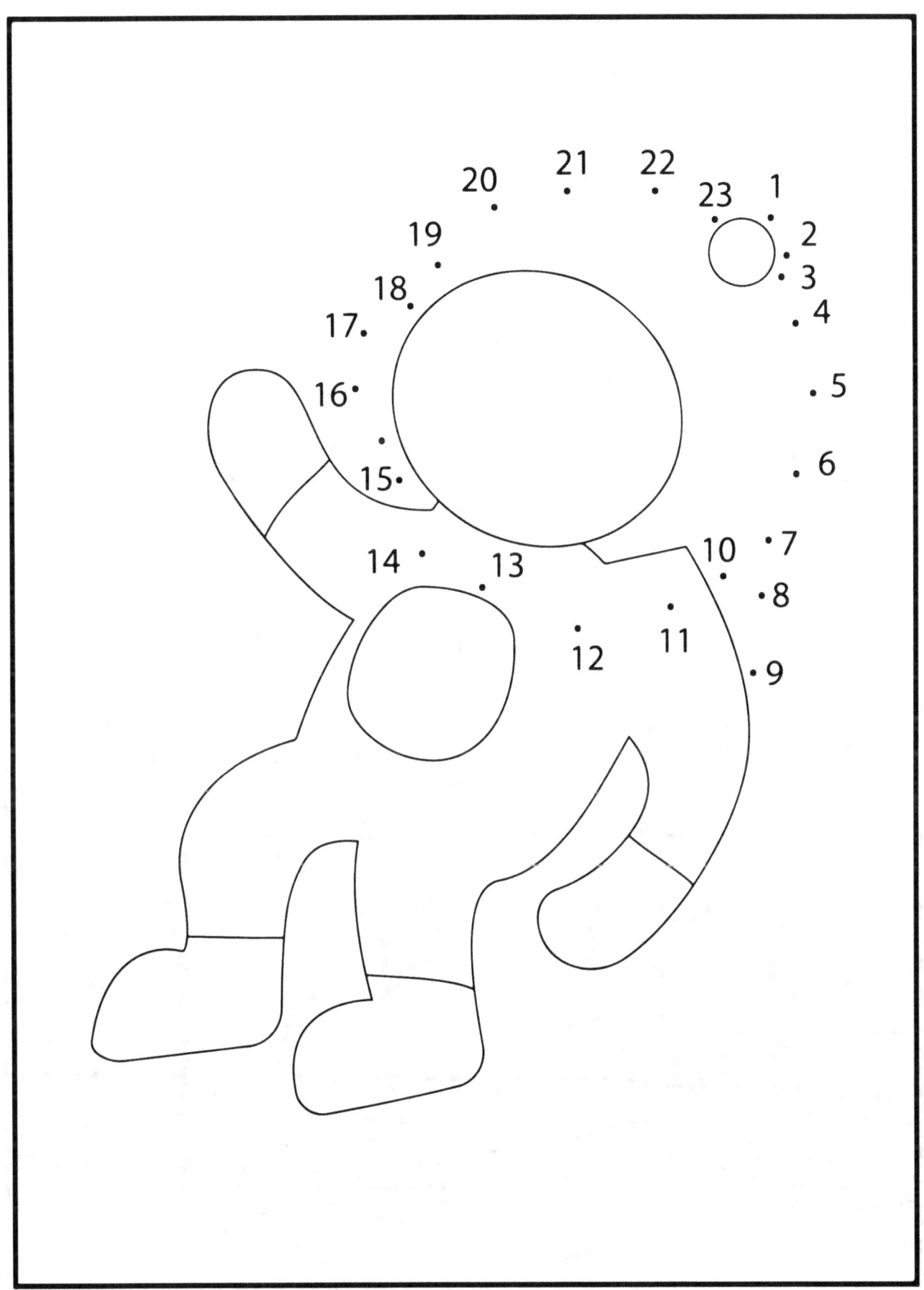

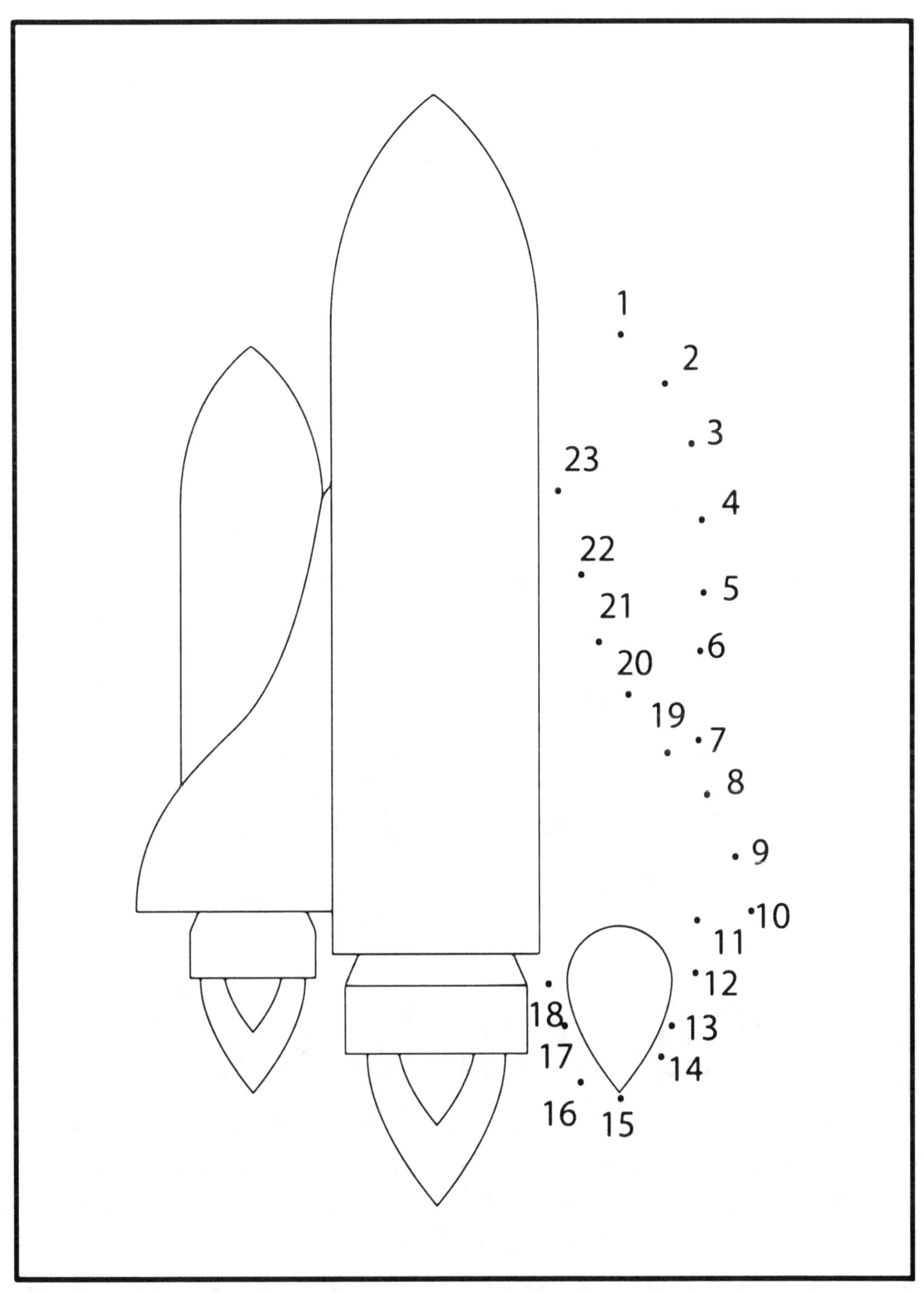

DID YOU KNOW?

Did you know that **some spaceships are faster than a bullet?** The fastest spaceship ever, **NASA's Parker Solar Probe,** can travel at 430,000 miles per hour—that's fast enough to go from **Earth to the Moon in just 40 minutes!**

HOW TO DRAW SPACE

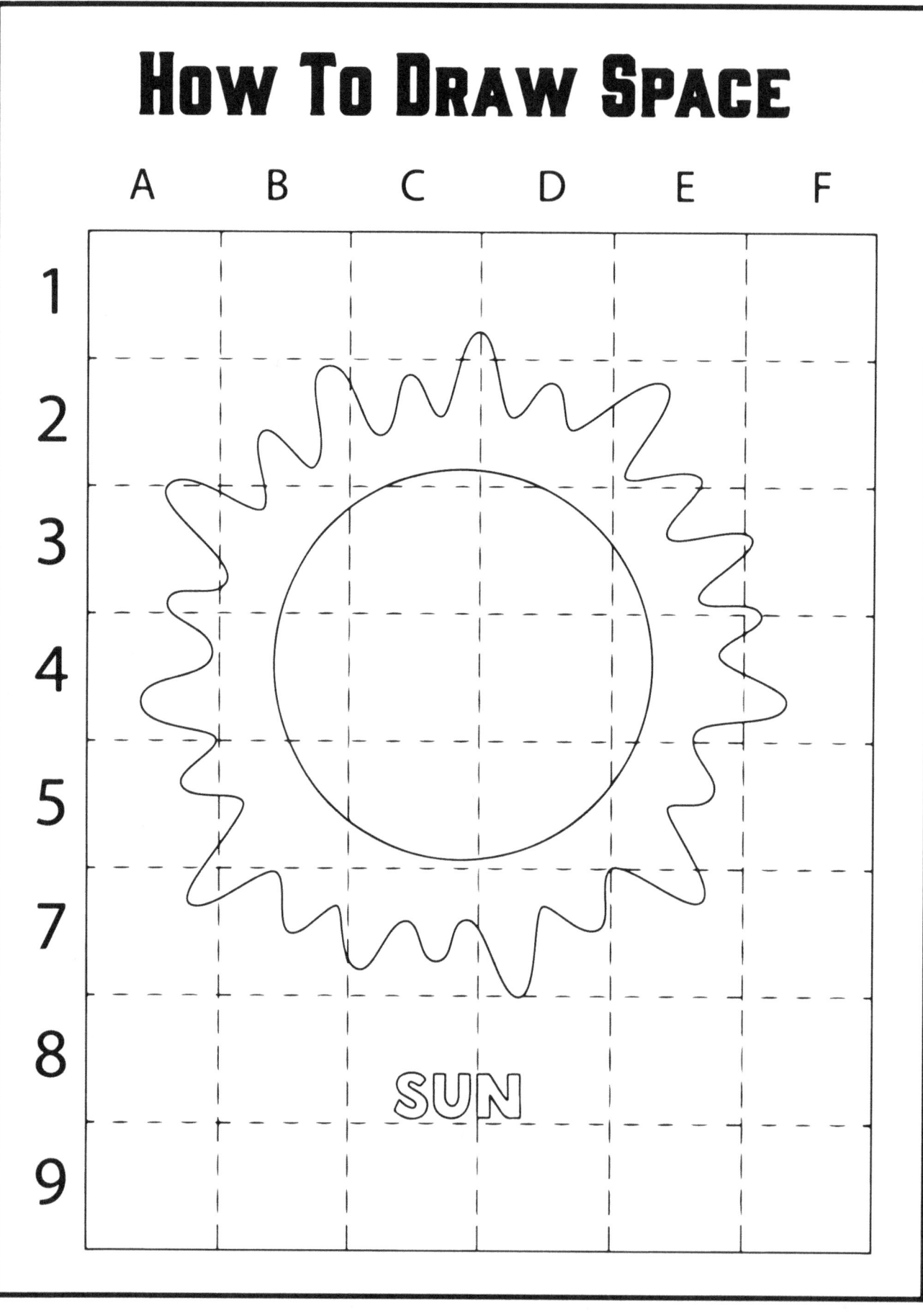

YOUR TURN!

	A	B	C	D	E	F
1						
2						
3						
4						
5						
7						
8						
9						

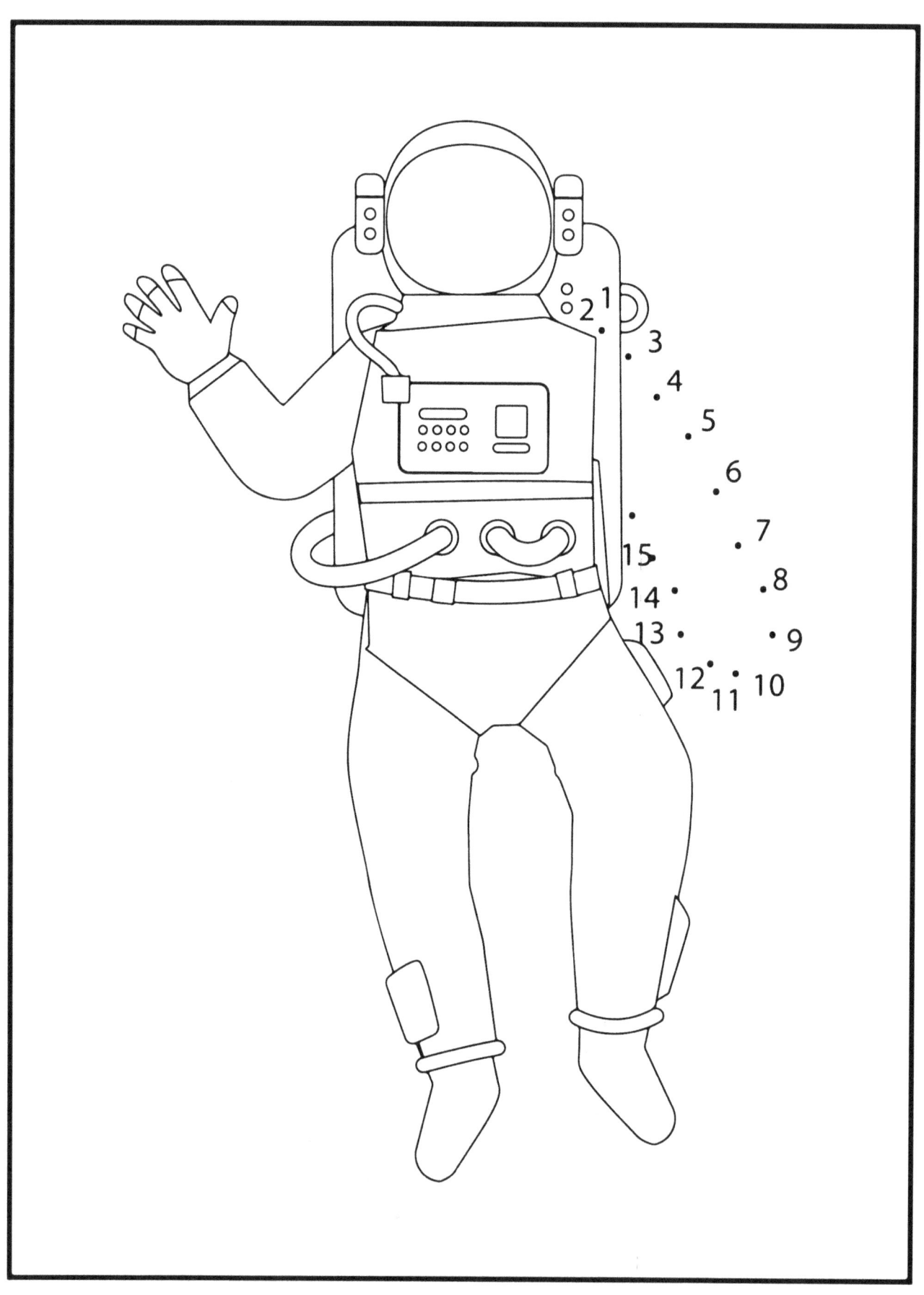

SPACE EXPLORER'S PACKING LIST!

Circle the correct things an astronaut would need for a space trip and cross out the wrong ones.

How To Draw Space

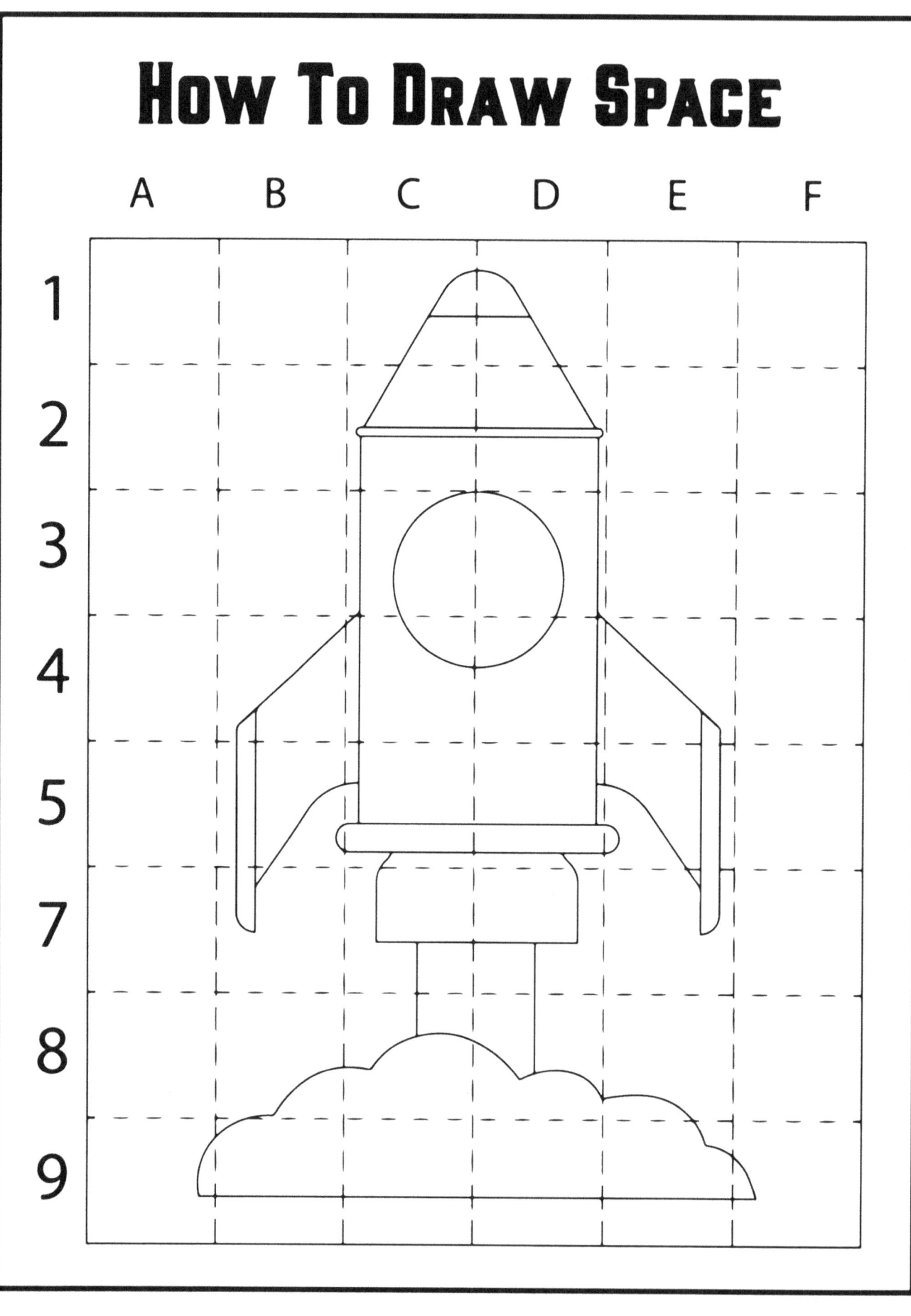

YOUR TURN!

	A	B	C	D	E	F
1						
2						
3						
4						
5						
7						
8						
9						

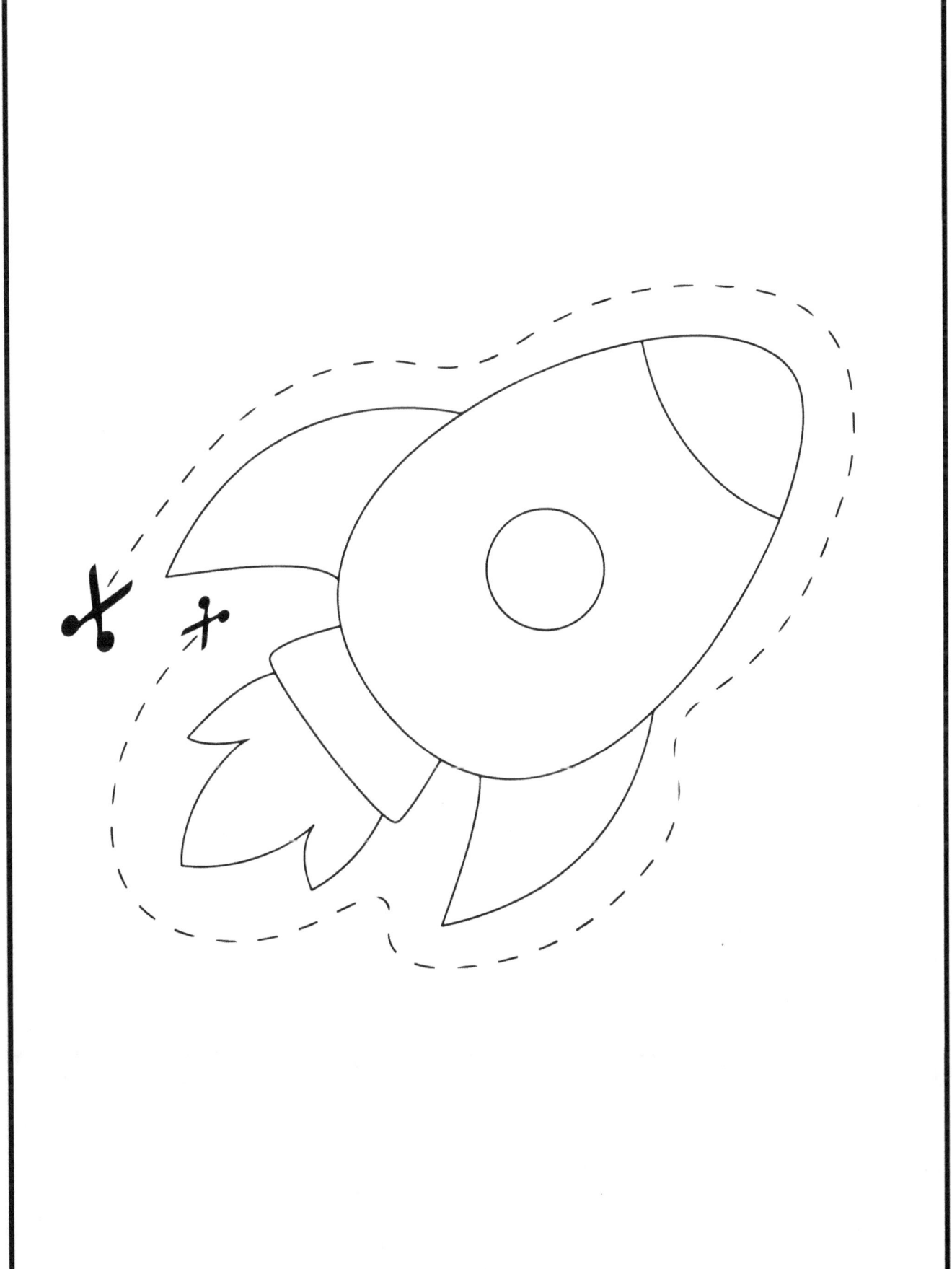

How To Draw Space

A B C D E F

1 2 3 4 5 7 8 9

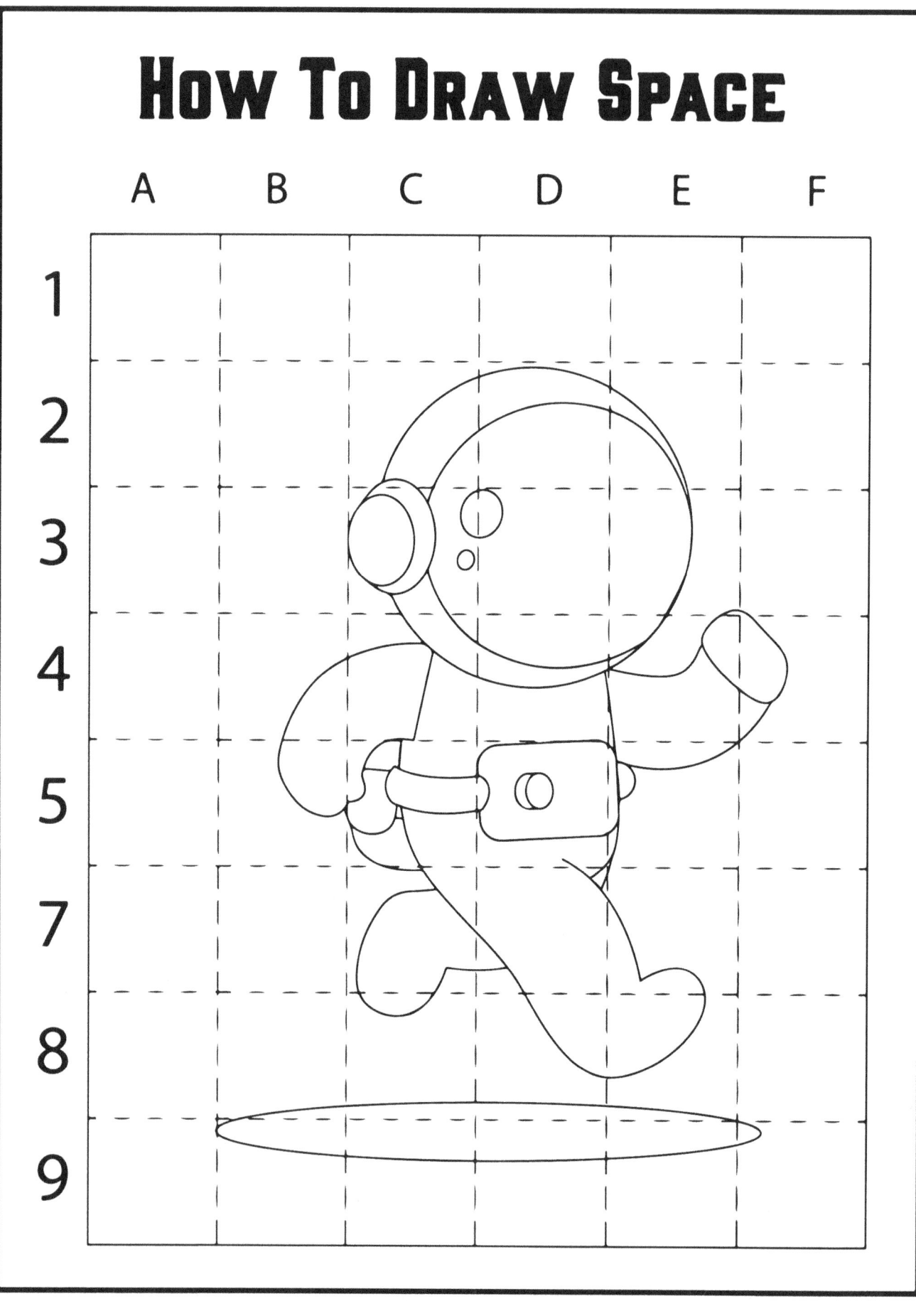

YOUR TURN!

	A	B	C	D	E	F
1						
2						
3						
4						
5						
7						
8						
9						

Dear Space Explorer,

Congratulations on reaching the final page of Space and Planets for Kids! You have completed an amazing journey through space, coloring planets, solving mazes, connecting the dots, and practicing your scissor skills. I am so proud of you for exploring the universe with creativity and curiosity!

Through this book, you have developed important skills. Coloring has helped you express your imagination and creativity while improving hand-eye coordination. Dot-to-Dot activities have sharpened your number skills and patience as you revealed hidden space pictures. Dot marker pages have given you a fun way to strengthen fine motor skills while making beautiful space art and   Scissor skills pages have helped you practice careful cutting, which improves hand control and coordination. Mazes have challenged your problem-solving skills, helping you think critically while having fun!

By finishing this book, you have shown dedication, creativity, and a love for learning. Keep exploring, keep imagining, and never stop reaching for the stars!

With cosmic congratulations,

Catherine Worren

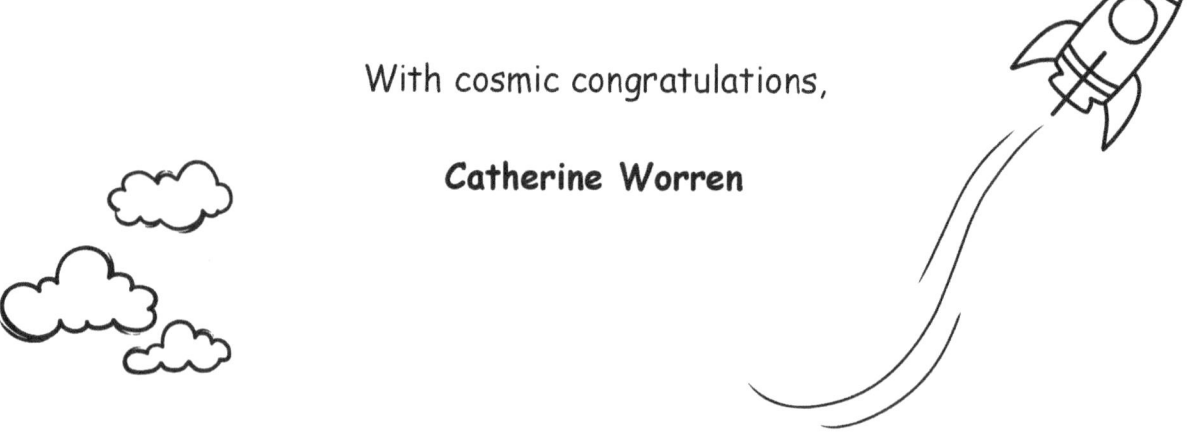

PS - If you enjoyed this book and find it to be a source of joy, encouragement, and growth, we kindly invite you to leave a review on Amazon. Your support will not only help us reach more children, but also inspire us to continue creating meaningful books.